Visser Publishing
2670 Harrison Blvd. • Ogden, Utah 84401

WHY I WROTE THIS BOOK!

This book is put together as a true field manual. Over the last 30 years, I have seen hundreds of treasure related books. A few of them had more than one subject in them. For instance, one would have some good treasure stories in it. Another might have a few stories and a few pages on how to read Spanish treasure symbols. Some would have how to pan for gold and some are about how to use the art of dowsing to find treasure. There are many others. You would have to buy seven or eight different books to really get started in treasure hunting!!

So that is why I have put together a field manual with all subjects needed to get started.

I also always wished that there were blank pages in the back of the book so I could make notes as I researched each story; that is now in my books.

The how-to chapters are short and basic. The goal of this book is to keep it simple, but still give plenty of information to get going and be successful.

Hopefully, all the spelling is correct. Some of the grammar is not. It is done purposefully; as I wanted the words to stay exactly the way I received them from the original sources, so as to not change the original flavor and feel of the stories. A large amount of information was given to me as a small kid in the early sixties. I have no idea where some of it came from. I know some were from very old magazines and newspapers. To make sure you don't get too serious, I put a few cartoons in that I copied when I was about ten years old; I still don't know exactly where they came from. I think they are very nifty! The names of any sources that I still know have been placed in the back of the book. Some info was from interviews I did later with old railroad men and miners in some rest homes. All of these men died over twenty years ago. I misplaced some of the names over the years. I had never intended to write books on treasure hunting; I wanted to go find the gold myself. I soon found out that one man can not look for so many places, so I decided to put 30 years of info into some books so maybe some others could look for the treasures. I am a collector of stories and histories of this great state. I also collect photos of old treasure marks on trees and rocks, as well as Indian markings. If you have any of the above that you would like to share, let me know! All things will be kept confidential. A big part of why I do this is to preserve history. Many times when I go back to see some old markings that I photographed, they have been destroyed by some brainless idiot shooting at them or carving their name over the old marks. Logging companies have destroyed many large sections of original old growth timber. On some of these old giants were names and dates from almost two hundred years ago. Now they are gone forever.

This book will take you to some of the best places in the state to find old mines and buried treasures. What a great way to spend time in the outdoors! Don't be too serious – have fun, take your time and go prepared.

Don't make or leave any messes. Always get permission to go on private land. You will have good luck and not get jinxed if you do not get greedy. Yes, I will take ten percent if this book helps you find something!!

Good luck and happy hunting!
David Visser

A STORY OF TREASURE FOUND

Long before he reached the place where he figured he would find the treasure he was after, Frank Fish felt it was going to be his lucky day. Even he, one of America's most accomplished amateur treasure hunters, could hardly have guessed how lucky.

As his jeep bounced along a rocky trail never intended for an automotive vehicle, Fish reviewed the research that had brought him to the Guadalupe Mountains of southern New Mexico. In an abandoned mining town he hoped to find the loot that he believed two robbers had buried there back in the 1880's. One of the outlaws had disappeared; the other had been captured and died in prison. Fish's research in books and other places, plus some previous digging at other likely sites had convinced him that he was now on the right track.

On the outskirts of the crumbling ghost town, he zeroed in on an arroyo, which, his calculations had finally told him, was the site of a shack once inhabited by the robbers. As he searched the area with his metal detector, it began signaling – metal underneath. After a few hours of hard digging, he had unearthed an assortment of items. On the tarp he had spread out beside the diggings, there were a number of coins dating from 1822 to 1877, a stone jug, some old locks and many keys. It was nothing like the treasure he sought, but Fish wasn't discouraged. He kept circling around the place where he had made these discoveries.

Soon, his metal detector gave another high sound and he began digging again. Two feet down, his shovel hit some bone fragments and, beneath them, a rusted Springfield rifle. Under the rifle, he made a gruesome find – a human skull with a bullet hole in it. Fish still did not stop digging because the detector indicated there was more metal below. Thirty inches farther down, the seeker hit his jackpot – a huge iron kettle.

Prying off the old stove lid that covered it, he beheld a mass of blackened gold and silver coins. Still more exciting was the pile of rectangular objects that lay under them. In a few minutes, he had recovered eleven solid silver bars. But, that was not all. At the bottom of the kettle, he found a dozen gold nuggets and two bags of gold dust.

His time and research paid off for Frank Fish and it can for you, too. This story from the 1970's is a good example of what can happen. With today's fancy electronic doodads, it is better than ever to spend time in this great hobby!

COLORADO

TABLE OF CONTENTS

Section 1:

STORIES

Frenchmen gold of Del Norte

Treasure Mountain is located in the gold and silver rich San Juan Mountains of Colorado. Find any old-timer in the area between Lake City and Del Norte and he will not only point the mountains out to you, but will probably tell you about the times he too has looked for the cave with the gold bullion, estimated to be worth five to thirty million dollars, stored in it.

The gold bars were mined and hidden by a group of Frenchmen totaling nearly three hundred in number. There were miners, geologists, laborers and soldiers, all under the leadership of a man named LeBlanc.

The large expedition left a Kansas post in the early 1800's for the Colorado Mountains by way of the Platte River. Once in the mountains they began prospecting and exploring, looking or that one gold vein that could make them all rich. As they passed through the mountains a small quantity of gold was mined at Cripple Creek, but nowhere could gold be found in sufficient quantities to warrant their setting up mining operations on a large scale. Nowhere, that is, until they arrived at Treasure Mountain. There the group found gold in large quantities and immediately set up mining operations. Whether they knew they were on Spanish land is not known. At any rate, they mined the gold and stacked the bars on Spanish soil. Fortunately, their operations went undetected or a battle would most certainly have ensued over the possession of the gold.

As winter approached, the mine was closed and the men walked to Taos, New Mexico, for the winter where they were accepted and treated well by the Spanish and Indians who resided there. The winter was exceptionally cold and harsh on the

Frenchmen. One by one they began dying from disease and starvation until over two hundred of their number had perished. Come spring, the survivors decided to return to the mine, gather up what gold they could carry, then close the entrance and start back toward Kansas.

Unfortunately, they were plagued with bad luck. Shortly after leaving Taos they were attacked by Indians. When the battle was over only about fifteen men were still alive. The tragic loss of so many of their comrades was too much for the remaining men, so they turned eastward and started the long trek back to Leavenworth, Kansas. Still being followed by the Indians, they were attacked again when they reached the Arkansas River. Only five survived this attack. The five men, now frightened to move on for fear they would all be killed, ran into the woods determined to stay hidden until the feared Indians were gone.

Their situation became so desperate finally that they drew straws, with the loser giving up his life so the others could stay alive by reverting to cannibalism. By the time the survivors managed to leave their hiding place and struggle overland to Leavenworth, they had been forced to draw two more times.

The two survivors who struggled into the fort were more dead than alive. One of them died a few hours later, and the sole survivor swore never to return to the mine and its gold. He had brought maps of the treasure site back with him and told anyone who would listen of the horrors of the trip.

As far as can be learned, no one was ever able to find the hidden gold and it still waits for some lucky treasure hunter.

Treasure of Juan Cruz

According to Indian legends gold was discovered on Spanish Peaks in what is now Huerfano County before white men came. A Spanish story tells of three monks and several other Spaniards who stayed behind in the area of Spanish Peaks when Coronado returned to Mexico after his ill-fated search for the mythical City's of Cibola.

Two of the monks were killed by Indians. The third one, Juan de la Cruz, with the other Spaniards, forced the Indians of the Pecos to mine and bring gold from the depths of the Twin Mountains. After several years, Juan Cruz and his men left the peaks with pack animals heavily loaded with gold, bound for Mexico City. They never arrived at their destination and it never learned what happened to them.

An incident occurred in 1811 that lends credence to the existence of these mines and legends. Gold nuggets that are believed to have been part of this treasure were found by a Mexican south of the double mountains, far from any mine or mineral-bearing ledges. With the price of gold today, it could pay an interested prospector to check the area of Spanish Peaks.

Bear Creek Gold

This story of a lost mine is unusual because it has been found and lost again three different times.

A prospector came to Durango, Colorado, one day in 1905, loaded down with the weight of a sackful of extremely rich ore. He was in urgent need of some ready money and could not wait for the ore to be smelted and returned from the Denver mint as coin. After having the specimens of the ore assayed, he showed the assayer's report and offered the sackful of ore for sale. While displaying it to possible cash customers, he related how he came by it.

When prospecting in the Bear Creek region of the eastern Nettleton district, he said, about 30 miles from Durango, he shad accidentally found the tunnel of an old mine. He realized some mystery hovered over the mine, for there was evidence that it had been abandoned suddenly, and probably involuntarily, many years before.

All around the floor and on the ground outside the tunnel, were heaps of gold ore, of the same kind he had in the sack. The ore was very high grade and the vein, which he did not take time to locate, being short of food, must have been only a few feet away. Inside the tunnel were the skeletons of three men, bleached snow-white, though covered with dust. The prospector cagily avoided telling any landmarks to get back to the tunnel.

The prospector was eager to sell the ore quickly return to the mine with an adequate supply of provisions and the necessary equipment to make a thorough survey of the extent of the gold vein. After selling his gold and buying supplies, the prospector left town and was never seen again.

In the late spring of 1918, a sheepherder brought into Durango a sack of gold ore which was recognized by old-timers as the same sort of rich ore brought in by Martinez. The sheepherder told the same tale, identical in all details.

Local people decided that a story checking three ways and standing up through so many years must have some basis in fact. Several townsmen grubstaked the sheepman to lead them to the Three Sheletons mine. The expedition was quickly begun and as quickly abandoned. The guide could not find the way back. The mine is believed to be around Bear Creek, Where it flows through the eastern Nettleton district, about thirty miles from Durango.

The Rusted Shovel Mine

Sometime between the years 1938 and 1940, three men were working on the highway a few miles north of Salida, Colorado. Work shut down for a few days so they decided to do a little prospecting in the nearby mountains, just to kill time.

They stumbled on an abandoned mine which looked as though the owner had either met with violence, or just walked off without ever returning. They wondered what had actually happened, as somebody had left badly rusted tools lying in the excavation. Maybe some prospector had just made the excavation and failed to locate ore rich enough, and walked off looking for a better vein.

Something didn't add up, so the three workers searched for some kind of clue that might explain why the mine had been abandoned. There were no graves close by to indicate the previous miner had died. Each tool was an antique, so whoever left them there, had done it a long time ago.

The three men took samples of ore. It looked good to them, however, an assay would soon tell whether it was worth working. For reasons unknown, the samples weren't sent to the assay office right away and when the returns came back, they proved the ore to be rich in gold.

However, not being miners and having good jobs, which they did not want to lose, the men followed another highway project to a different area and soon forgot about the gold. They later told the story but never searched for the mine.

Since it happened within the last fifty years, this location certainly bears further investigation. And by doing local research, this little known lost mine just might be fund by a persevering prospector.

The Mystery of Cripple Creek

This "lead" is for those treasure hunters who are interested in solving a mystery through local research concerning a particular site.

In 1858, gold was discovered in Colorado, and by 1859, 50,000 prospectors had flocked to the state. The area around Cripple Creek was one particular area that attracted many of these hunters.

When the gold was shipped from Cripple Creek, it was often sent down the Gold Camp road on the south side of Pike's Peak. But sometimes; however, it was sent round the north side of Pike's Peak and through Ute Pass, a 6,800 foot-high pass near Manitou Springs. In those days it was a dark and brooding place, with pine and aspen trees overshadowing the winding trail used by travelers.

In 1873, a stagecoach carrying five passengers and $40,000 in gold entered the pass. The sun was shining and everything seemed perfectly normal. But the stagecoach was never seen again!

The coach, the driver, five passengers, team and the $40,000 in gold simply disappeared. There was never any trace found of any of them.

For the mystery bluff, this location should prove to be a challenge.

Falls Creek Cache

In late October 1903, Henry Sommers was walking the trail from the Neglected Mine on Monument Mountain to Durango, Colorado, about twenty miles to the southeast. Near the head of Falls Creek he noticed the corner of a canvas sack sticking out from under a rock. Henry had found a hi-grader's cache.

There were twelve sacks, each weighing sixty pounds. Removing the sacks, Sommers carried them about three hundred yards away, where he buried them carefully in a small natural trench.

Not wanting to leave a marker, Henry made a careful note of landmarks. To the right was a white sandstone cliff, another cliff stood out on the left, opposite the burial site. A large dead tree was across the canyon. These three landmarks formed a triangle with the cache in the center.

After reaching Durango he met tow miners who seemed to be the hi-graders. Although he couldn't prove it, Sommers felt the two men were watching him. Deciding to wait, Sommers got a job and spent the winter in Durango. By the following summer the two hi-graders had left town.

Henry returned to the cache site but was unable to locate the gold. After searching several days, Sommers gave up. He told several people about the cache then moved on west. This would be a good location to search with a metal detector.

Look for a small ditch, probably sunken more by now, between a white sandstone cliff and another cliff, opposite each other near the head of Falls Creek, northwest of Durango.

Two Brothers Mine

Two brothers, Eli and Red Hansen, discovered a rich vein of gold ore in Moffat County, Colorado. They worked the mien for several months, then after concealing all signs of their work, started out for supplies. Just as they reached the Utah state line, they were killed by bushwhackers.

Afraid they would be caught, after searching the bodies and finding only a small amount of gold, the Bushwhackers buried the two dead men. What gives this story a ring of truth is the statement made to a friend by and old-time farmer in the area, now deceased, named Harry Chew.

In his own words here is why he believed the mine existed:

I'll tell you what I found and what makes me a dead sure about the mine and maybe a cache of gold, because them Hansen brothers had been working the mine for quite a while. Some years ago I was exploring a steep cliff in Pool Canyon. I saw an odd shaped rock, when I picked it up it was a human skull. I did some more digging and found two bodies, on one skull was some red hair, same color as Red Hansen had. The last time I saw the Hansen brothers had been about two years before I found the bodies.

I had been chasing a mountain lion and came across the Hansens. They weren't friendly and seemed to want me to leave. Nobody never heard of them anymore until I found the two bodies."

Harry had searched for the mine and believed that the Hansens had cached a lot of gold near the mine. Chew found prospect holes, shallow shafts and several rusted picks and shovels, but he could never locate the hidden mine. Until his death, Henry Chew always believed that the mine and gold cache existed in Pool Canyon.

Devil's Head Gold

For years the area around Devil's Head, in the foothills of the Rocky Mountains between Denver and Colorado Springs was used by different outlaw gangs as a hideout.

In 1923, a forest ranger named Roy Dupree noticed an old man who had pitched a tent and seemed to be looking for something. Inviting him to the station, Dupree asked him what he was searching for. The old man told a strange tale.

He said that one day in 1870 a gang of robbers held up a government pay roll near Big Springs and collected $60,000 in gold coins. The outlaws headed for the Devil's Head area. However, before they reached it the posse closed in on the outlaws and a deadly battle ensued. The desperate robbers buried the gold under a pine tree and rove a knife into the tree as a marker. Only one of the bandits managed to escape.

The old man told the ranger that he was the man who had escaped. He said that for many years he had been in prison for another robbery. Now he had returned to look for the buried gold.

Dupree told the old man that a forest fire had ravaged the area during the intervening years. A new forest had grown up, and there would be no knife handle sticking out of any of those trees.

After searching for several days and finding nothing, the old man left. This would be a good place to spend a few days searching with a metal detector.

Lost Spaniards Mine

Almost everybody in southern Colorado, through five generations, has heard of the rich lost gold mine high in the nearby mountains. Spaniards came up from Mexico, a few years after the American Revolutionary War, and discovered, in a rugged mountain peak somewhere near what is now the state's southern border, an immensely rich deposit of gold.

The Spaniards began preparations for mining, timbering a shaft, making melting ovens and a cleaning trough. They had little more than started taking out ore, when something, never explained, occurred to call them away. They ordered their peons and Indian slaves to cover the mouth of the shaft and remove all evidence of their labor. Then destroying their trail down the mountainside, the Spaniards and their train of horses, mules and servants left the region forever.

There is no question that the mountains and mesas of Colorado are teeming with gold, but of the hundreds who have heard this legend, many have not believed it, thinking it wouldn't hold water. According to tradition, the Spaniards discovered the gold by accident, under conditions in which they were not equipped to undertake extensive and long continued mining operations.

Many old-timers who have hunted this lost lode believe it lies in the rugged peaks rising west of Trinidad as the southern point and Walsenburg as the northern point. Trinidad is in Las Animas County and Walsenburg is in Huerfano County.

Carrasco Rodriquez Treasure

Around 1700, the members of a Spanish regiment of soldiers buried between $50,000 and $1,000,000 in gold doubloons to avoid its capture by Apache Indians. The story is that an infantry regiment, commanded by Carrasco Rodriquez and carrying twelve chests of treasure, started from Santa Fe en route to a Spanish garrison at Saint Augustine, Florida.

Distaining guides, Rodriquez and his men marched in the wrong direction. Winter found them at the present site of Trinidad, where they waited until spring. Again straying in the wrong direction, they entered Purgatory River Canyon, where, according to a dying Apache's story told five years later in a Santa Fe mission, they were set upon and murdered by Indians.

The Indians witnessed the alarmed Spaniards leaving their treasure chests, but paid little heed, for they were satisfied with a loot of horses, blankets and rum. The treasure is believed to be still waiting for some lucky treasure hunter.

Dutch Oven Gold

In 1857, a wagon heavily loaded with $100,000 in gold bars and gold dust was winding its way from Denver to Missouri. The trail was hot, dusty and monotonous, all of which added to the boredom of the men driving the wagon. The boredom ended, however, quite suddenly. As the wagon rounded a curve, there in the middle of the road were several masked men. The drivers were ordered to hold their hands high and no harm would come to them. Neither man wanted to become a hero, especially a dead one, sot they readily complied. The bandits took the boxes holding the gold off the wagon, and thanking the drivers for stopping, sent them on their way with the suggestion that they don't stop until reaching the next settlement. Feeling lucky to still be alive, they had no intention of stopping.

The next settlement had a small military detachment garrisoned there for protection from the Indians. Upon hearing of the robbery, the commanding officer sent all the men he could spare out to try and recover the gold. Early the next morning, after traveling hard, the bandits were spotted. The bandits saw the soldiers coming through and rode in behind some rocks to make a stand. Realizing the heavy gold would slow them down, one man was chosen to find a hiding place and bury it. Placing all the gold in a Dutch oven, he slipped away from the area without being seen. Riding to within a mile of the Smokey hill Trail near the old town site of Clifford, he buried the oven about two feet deep. To mark the spot, he carved the date into three large flat stones and placed them in the shape of a triangle with the treasure in the center.

He then rode back to the scene of battle to try and help his friends, but he was too late. They were all dead. Scared that he too would be found and killed, he turned his horse and left the area as rapidly as possible.

Nothing more was heard about the hidden gold until the late 1880's, when the lone survivor returned to try and recover the treasure. He spent days looking but time had dimmed his memory and changed the country. He was unable to find the location. Before returning to Chicago, he told several people what he had been looking for and asked to be remembered if anyone found the gold.

No one, however, was ever able to locate the three stones, so the little Dutch oven still waits, two feet underground, to be discovered.

Big Badly Cache

In the summer of 1860, two Missourians trekked to the gold country in Summit County, Colorado, expecting to strike it rich. Seasoned prospectors in the area laughed at the two young greenhorns' inexperienced efforts.

The old-timers got a big surprise when the Missourians began packing out large bags of strange gold-bearing white clay from some unknown source. Every night the two would disappear over the ridge, returning at dawn with their heavy bags of clay. For every 100 pounds of clay they were panning out an ounce of gold. The other miners wondered where the rich clay was coming from, but nobody wanted to tangle with the muscular, well-armed Missourians.

Finally, Jim Jorgensen's curiosity got the best of him. He followed the two Missourians one moonlit night while they skirted the top of Big Baldy Mountain. From there, he figured he could easily locate their claim later.

The Missourians worked until the cold winter halted all mining operations in the area. Then the Civil War broke out and they left, going back to Missouri and never returned.

This was Jorgensen's chance. He organized a search party, confident they'd find the rich clay deposit, but the search failed, as all have since. The exact site of this rich gold deposit remains a secret to this day, though it has to be somewhere in the vicinity of Big Baldy Mountain in Summitt County, Colorado

Ute Gold

Around 1851, a pack train of five white men and seven mules, with five of the mules carrying two sacks of gold each, was heading eastward from California to join the Santa Fe Train in New Mexico. Circling south of what is now Durango, Colorado, across Florida Mesa into the Ignacio Mountains, the train was deep in Ute Indian territory.

Unexpectedly the party came upon a small Indian hunting camp. The men decided to skirt the village to avoid trouble, but the smell of cooking meat led two of them to dismount and gather a supply of it for supper.

As the men were remounting one horse shied, knocking over a tepee. Hurrying to catch up with the train, they did not notice that the tepee had fallen over a campfire. The camp was soon destroyed.

That night the party camped along the Piedra River, opposite the mouth of the Stolsteimer, with Chimney Rock off the northeast.

Early the next morning, while one of the men was catching the stock, the Utes surprised the camp, killing four of the men. The fifth man, who witnessed the massacre, ran for cover and escaped.

The Indians rifled the camp and took everything of value, except the 10 sacks of gold. They had no use for the gold and dumped it into a shallow ravine nearby, where it still lies, probably covered by dirt washed down by rains.

Strong Box Cache

An event that happened near Clifford Colorado, took place in 1862. By this time the country was becoming more populated and less dangerous to live in. Several small short-run stage lines had been started to carry supplies between the new settlements springing up everywhere. One such stage was making its run from Fairplay to Ute Pass. The only thing being carried was a strong box containing $80,000 in gold coin.

As the stage pulled into the Como area, ten bandits jumped out from both sides of the road and ordered the driver to stop. Unfortunately, the driver was not about to give up the shipment to any group of bandits and gave the team a crack with his whip. Before he had time to swing his whip twice one of the bandits shot and killed him. The guard was not about to try anything foolish. He stopped the stage and threw down his rifle. The bandits took the gold and sent the stage on its way with the usual warning, "Don't look back."

The guard found help in the next town and a posse was quickly formed and set out in pursuit of the bandits. The chase came to an end when the bandits were caught near the old town site of Clifford. While two of their number buried the strongbox, the rest were keeping the posse busy. One by one, though, the bandits were being killed by the posse's extremely accurate rifle fire. The battle lasted several hours before the last bandit was finally shot.

When the posse rushed to the scene, all ten men were either dead or dying. The men of the posse searched everywhere for the gold but were unable to find a trace of it, and sadly enough, al of the bandits died without revealing where the strongbox had been

hidden

Needless Mountain Stash

In the summer of 1893, Tom Estes, a miner and prospector, discovered a rich vein of gold somewhere on the slopes of West Needles Mountain in the San Juan Range of southwestern Colorado.

During his first summer of mining the vein, Estes filled two sacks with rich sylvanite ore, which netted him $1,070. The following summer he packed the mountains a large supply of tools, including an anvil, bellows and blacksmith's coal. He came out with seven sacks of ore and told friends it had taken him only two days to dig it out. The remainder of his time at the mine had been spent, he said, in timbering the tunnel, covering a shaft and building a forge.

Estes also built a permanent camp, expecting to spend his summers in the mountains and returning with only enough gold for a necessary stake. Apparently, gold stored in a mountain appeared to him as safer than it would be in any bank.

Estes stayed only two weeks at his mine during the third summer. He came out with five packs of ore, which he sold for $2,800.

The following winter Estes died of pneumonia. He left no map or other directions to his mine. All that is known is that the miner went up Cascade Creek into Purgatory Canyon before picking his way up the rugged mountainside on the north.

Neither the source of the rich ore he brought out of the mountains nor the gold he is believed to have stored there has been discovered.

Trinket Gold

The Colorado Rockies are noted for their rugged beauty, their ski slopes, and in the case of one of the "fourteeners," for treasure.

A fourteener to a native of Colorado is any mountain over fourteen thousand feet high, and there are over 50 in the state. This treasure tale concerns Mt. Princeton, in the Collegiate Range.

The braves were gone when the Spaniards stole all of the gold trinkets in the village. But they returned, learned what had happened and gave chase. As the Indians got closer, the thieves were forced to lighten their load and cached two calfskins full of gold just below the chalk cliffs of Mt. Princeton.

The Spaniards never revealed the site of the cache because the Indians caught up with them and slaughtered them. The Indians were unable to find their gold trinkets, which had been stolen from them.

Irish Mine

The Cache la Poudre River (the name is French for hiding place of powder) rises in Rocky Mountain National Park. It flows north, then turns east and southeast through Fort Collins and Greeley, eventually emptying into the South Platte River.

In the early days, when Fort Collins was a real fort, two unnamed prospectors, one an Irishman and the other a Dutchman, came into the fort regularly and cashed their supply of gold at the Settler's post. These trips always ended in prolonged drunken sprees, after which they would quietly leave.

Each trip to the fort by the prospectors produced more gold and it became common knowledge that the two men were working a rich mine somewhere in the area, although they never got drunk enough to reveal its location. On one occasion some inquisitive soldiers hired an Indian scout to follow the miners. The scout returned some days later and reported that he had followed the men straight up the Cache la Poudre for three days and had then lost their trail.

On a subsequent trip to the fort the partners got drunk as usual and quarreled. In the brawl that resulted the Irishman killed the Dutchman. The soldiers, now determined to make the Irishman talk, strung him up to a tree, not intending to kill him. But when the prospector was brought down, he was dead. The secret of the mine died with him.

Henry Huff's Gold

Bull Canyon, somewhat north of the four Corners country of southwestern Colorado, is the location of a considerable sum of treasure in gold and silver coins, gold dust and nuggets. The treasure is well known...even the State of Colorado has searched for it. The exact value of the cache, or caches, is not known precisely, but at least $5,500 in gold coins is involved. That much is a matter of public record.

The treasure was once the secreted fortune of Henry Huff, who was shot and killed by John Keski at Keski's house in 1917. The two men quarreled in the presence of Mrs. Keski and their two children. Carl Akers, Henry Huff's partner and only friend, was also present.

When Keski mortally wounded Henry Huff, they dying man dictated his will. He left all of his possession, including his buried gold, to his friend Akers. However, he did not survive long enough to give the location of his hoard.

When Akers tried to claim the estate as the sole heir, he found that the state of Colorado would not recognize deathbed wills, and that the state claimed the inheritance.

It did not make any difference, however, since not even the state could locate Henry Huff's treasure hoard. No one else seems to have had any better luck, or if they have, they have kept it to themselves. Carl Akers searched, as did others, but Huff's gold has not been found as far as it is known.

Bull Canyon runs east of the Dolores River and is south of the Colorado towns of Bedrock and Naturita in Montrose County. Until recently Huff's old cabin remained standing, and the U.S. Geological Survey has a photograph of it.

Dead man's Creek Mine

A blinding blizzard caught three prospectors by surprise high in the Sangre de Cristo Range of Sagauch County, Colorado, in October of 1880. The three men, S.J. Harkman, E.R. Oliver and H.A. Melton, hurriedly sought refuge in a cave they found near the head of Dead Man's Creek.

Once inside, the three men lit dry pine branches for torches and began to explore their shelter. A narrow tunnel, ten or twelve feet long, led to a large room. They followed a second rough passageway into a larger room. It appeared empty until Oliver Kicked something with his foot – a skull!

They fashioned fresh torches to do more exploring. In a smaller chamber with many stone ledges their curiosity was unexpectedly rewarded. They found five gold bars stacked neatly beneath one of the ledges.

Impatiently, the men waited out the storm, then made their way back to camp with the treasure. Being sure there were more gold bars hidden in the cave, each had made careful mental notes of its exact location. They were experienced prospectors, familiar with the territory, and so anticipated no problem in returning to the cave the following spring.

But problems were all they found when they returned. They were sure they had located the right canyon, but somehow the cave opening had disappeared, and they were never able to find it.

Indian Ridge Gold

Back in the early days of this century, gold and silver were still being taken out of mines around Creede, Silverton and Telluride, Colorado. High-grading (a fancy name for stealing) was not considered a sin unless you were caught. This explains how some of the riches gold ore ever taken out of the Colorado Rockies – ore valued at $120,000 on today's market – came to e cached at a place called Indian Ridge near the little town of Rico, Colorado.

Two men and a boy buried the ore one summer around 1910 and were never able to find it again. The two men were miners and the boy was a sheepherder, but he was important to the operation because he provided the mules to carry the 12 sacks of ore, which weighed about 70 pounds apiece.

In the dead of the night, one man and the boy started out with the mules. The other rode the train to the end of the line, where he planned to meet them. When he met them atop Indian Ridge there was trouble afoot. The sheriff and others were looking for them.

Hurriedly, the ore was buried. They thought they had the place marked well, but discounted the changes wrought by the high mountain winters. When the deep snow melts, it slides off the mountains and takes everything with it.

When the three came back to find the rich ore, the markers were all gone. The miners both died soon after, and the boy was never able to find the gold cache.

Slate Mountain Lost Mine

In the spring of 1849, Buck Rogers led a party of Illinois prospectors to the gold fields of California. When the men reached the Colorado Mountains they did a little side-prospecting to break the monotony of the long journey.

Rogers and five others found a rich strike in the Camp Fulford-Glenwood Springs are, but kept it a secret from the rest of the group. Furthermore, the six men remained behind when the party resumed the trek to California.

When fall came, Rogers and his partners had accumulated a hoard of gold valued at from $60,000 to $100,000, which was kept hidden near their camp. In the early winter, Rogers took about $500 of the hoard and set out for supplies. Upon reaching civilization, Rogers spent two weeks with convivial friends before heading back to the camp with supplies. When he arrived he found that the camp, men and gold had completely disappeared under a giant snow and earth slide.

Rogers never recovered from the shock. He became a broken alcoholic, drifting from saloon to saloon and babbling of the friends and fortune he had lost on "Slate Mountain," which was unknown and probably had been named by Rogers himself. He could – and would – give only general directions to the site, and the legend of the Lost Slate Mountain grew and spread.

A few years later, a doctor obtained directions to Slate Mountain that an old miner had made when he found what he believed was Slate Mountain. He made several attempts to find the lost gold, but never succeeded.

Here are the directions used by the doctor in his attempts to find Slate Mountain.:

Go along Eagle River to the mouth of Brush Creek. Follow Creek five miles to the forks. Take east branch about five miles until you come to a shift of rocks coming almost at water's edge. Follow dry gulch running north until you come to a small hole dug in the ground.

Continue on until you come to another hole, and so on, until you come to a third hole. This line is also marked by blazed trees on both sides. From the third hole turn due north and about 200 feet from the last tree you will see three tall trees standing in a triangle. The trees have their tops broken off about 30 feet up. This is about 300 feet from the timberline, and the vein runs north and south on the place described

Just after the turn of the century, a man named Hollingsworth was deer hunting in Colorado's rugged La Plate Mountains. While tracking a big buck he noticed an interesting outcropping. A prospector and miner, Hollingsworth couldn't pass it up, and stopped long enough to break off a sample.

Weeks later, Hollingsworth happened to run across the ore sample in his jacket pocket. He had forgotten all about it. Examining it more closely, he suddenly realized it was probably the riches find he had ever made.

The melting snows had scarcely receded from the mountains before Hollingsworth was hiking up Root Creek, where he had been hunting the previous fall when he discovered his rich ledge of gold. He was able to retrace his steps easily, even as far as finding the remains of the buck he had killed, in the vicinity of the rich ore. But search as he might, he couldn't pinpoint the exact spot where he had found the sample.

Hollingsworth knew the outcropping was on a sharp ridge between Root Creek and Snowslide Gulch. But though he searched extensively, he was unable to find his lost ledge.

Tokens of Victor

In 1891, the first gold mines just southwest of Pike's Peak in central Colorado were opened, and the towns of Cripple Creek and Victor sprang up around the diggings in short order.

During this same period America was faced with a severe shortage of coins, with the western states particularly affected. To alleviate this shortage many private individuals, bankers, merchants and assayers coined their own tokens. In 1900, a man named Joseph Lesher, who lived in Victor, began making odd octagonal tokens called Lesher Referendum Dollars. When presented to merchants and tradesmen, these were redeemed in goods and services, and sometimes currency, when available. The coins worked well in the city Victor's routine business, and Lesher struck more of them in 1901.

Zachary Hutton, a local cobbler, completely misunderstood the purpose of the Lesher Dollars. Instead of recognizing them as a strict barter coins, he hoarded them away as though they were genuine U.S. coins. He equated these dollars with real money, believing they would always be valuable. Just as he had done when real coins were plentiful, he scrupulously saved his money.

Victory was still in the grip of winter when Hutton died of pneumonia in 1902. Though some people searched, two tins that Hutton had stored his Lesher Dollars in could never be found.

Huttons's store of tokens still lies hidden in some nook amount the scattered foundations of Victor's crumbling buildings. How these funny, eight-sided coins are quite rare, worth up to $1,000 each to collectors.

Swamp Silver

One portion of the road from Silverton to del Norte, Colorado, crossed Timber Hill. The hill was heavily wooded and so steep that the horses had to slow to a walk. This made it a favorite spot for those who planned to rob either the stage or ore wagons.

Many are the tales of treasure hidden in the area. One concerns the attempted hijacking of three ore wagons. Three scouts riding ahead of the wagons were ambushed, but one scout managed to carry a warning back to the wagons.

The drivers threw the sacks of silver ore into a swamp, not far from Timber hill. They managed to unload two wagons but before they could unload the third wagon, the bandits attacked..

The hijackers got only the silver from one wagon. The sacks of silver ore from the other two wagons were never recovered and are believed to still be in the swamp.

Section 2:

TREASURE TROVE LAW

This section is short and to the point. Be very careful and do not talk to anyone about finds until you totally check out all laws.

The Right to Search on Private Land

To search on private property, obviously the first thing the treasure hunter must do is get permission from the owner of the property. Although this permission is often given verbally, any seasoned treasure hunter, whether he's seeking a jackpot treasure or simply bottles and coins, prefers a written agreement with the property owner. In general, such an agreement should include the following:

1) A statement about the reason for digging.
2) A statement concerning the ownership and/or division of any treasure found.
3) A guarantee that the searcher will leave the property in the condition in which he found it. (In other words, he'll fill in the holes he digs.)
4) A disclaimer of liability on the part of the property owner if the treasure hunter meets with an accident while searching for the treasure.

If you write out your own agreement, as many treasure hunters do, you should make at least one carbon copy. Searcher and property owner should each sign both copies.

Ready-made forms are available at various metal detector and treasure hunter supply stores. Many clubs provide them for their members.

The Right to Search on Public Lands

Some areas of public land, federal and state, are absolutely barred to treasure hunters. National Parks and most State Parks are in this category. National Forest, in general, are open to treasure hunters, but new regulations are being formulated in regard to some National Forest lands. You should check with the office of the particular forest in which you intend to search, or with one of the regional offices listed elsewhere in this Information Center.

The Bureau of Land Management, which owns millions of acres of land (the amount changes, due to sale or transfer of some of it to other governmental units), in general has no restrictions on treasure hunting on BLM land.

Sunken Treasure

Inasmuch as most of our readers will not be going after this type of treasure, we will not attempt to deal extensively with it here. The laws pertaining to salvage are complex, and the rules in regard to ownership or rights to the valuables found aboard sunken ships are too difficult to summarize briefly. We recommend Salvage Law from Sunken Ships to Outboards, a handy little manual that will give you most of the basic facts.

Who Owns Treasure You May Find

If you find a treasure trove, can you keep it? This question has had varied answers in the courts, which have heard many disputes. Some cases in the U.S. have resulted in legal definitions that tend to set up the rule of "finders keepers."

Today your right to keep treasure you find, or to carry out any agreed-upon split with the owner of the property on which you find it, is modified by state laws. Each year more states are passing laws which govern the disposition of treasure. Such laws are generally referred to as "Antiquities Acts." Louisiana's Act 172 is an example. It reads, in part:

Florida has a law entitling it to one-fourth of the proceeds from any treasure found there. It is necessary in this state, as in some others, to obtain a license.

Regulation of treasure hunting and its proceeds is an area which is subject to an increasing number of laws, so the situation in any given state may change. An excellent general source of information on recent laws is A.T. Evans's Treasure Hunter's Yearbook. It is published early in each calendar year and contains a section on "Law and the Treasure Hunter." A copy may be ordered directly from the publisher, Eureka Press, Odessa, Texas 79760. The price is $4.00 postpaid.

Specific local information pertaining to your state or locality can be obtained at local metal detector dealers, rock shops, and treasure hunter and rockhound clubs.

Taxes

Two questions often asked by treasure hunters:
"Can I deduct expenses connected with treasure hunting?"
"What taxes do I have to pay on treasure I find?"

We won't attempt to go into the whole complex matter of income taxes. The IRS has changed the rules, and its interpretations of the rules, many times. So before you actually file a tax return, you had better check with the IRS for its latest thinking on this matter.

We can present you with a few general rules, however. The basic one pertaining to deductions for expenses connected with a hobby--any hobby, not just treasure hunting--is that you are entitled to deduct expenses equivalent to the income you derive from it. In other words, if you expenses connected with treasure hunting were $800 in a given year and in that year you found treasure worth $500, you could list $500 as expenses, and you wouldn't pay taxes on that amount.

If you're conducting your treasure hunting as a business, with the full intention of earning money from it, you can deduct all legitimate expenses--even gasoline needed to get you to treasure sites, lodgings while you hunt for the treasure, etc. Metal detectors, gold extracting equipment, scuba gear, books, and possibly even a four-wheel-drive vehicle are deductible expenses.

As to taxes you pay on treasure you find that how much they are and when you pay them depends on the kind of treasure. If what you find is gold (other than nuggets) or currency, the IRS quite naturally views it as income and takes a dim view of anyone who doesn't count is as such. However, if your treasure is in the form of bottles, barbed wire, or other collectors' items, a different situation pertains. Suppose you find a bottle that is worth $200, but you don't sell it. It's not, in the ordinary course of things, counted as income. It becomes income only if and when you do sell it.

Whatever its nature, if your find should be a big one, you can simply keep it and dole it out to yourself, counting as income only that portion of it turned into cash in any given year. Even if your find is in the form of currency, it is sometimes possible to arrange to spread out the income from it over a period of five years, under the IRS rules for "income averaging."

But we say again: Don't take our word for any tax information. Consult with the IRS or your own tax expert.

Section 3:

ANTIQUITIES LAW

This is just a small taste of how complicated and crazy these laws are. A tiny, small amount of bad people in the 1960's and 1970's destroyed some very important and historical sites. Now, a few people like this have ruined the relic-hunting hobby for thousands of people. Before, the laws were too open; how they have <u>over-reacted.</u> The laws are completely and totally unusable by anyone. According to state law, no one can pick up or collect anything-ever-no matter where they found it for fear of going to prison or being fined. Very, very sad and very wrong. So, be very careful about what you do and say! Always get permission and check the laws.

Utah Code Section 9-8-305

9-8-305. Permit required to survey or excavate on state lands — Ownership of collections and resources — Revocation or suspension of permits — Criminal penalties.
(1) (a) Before any person may survey or excavate for archaeological resources on any lands owned or controlled by the state or its subdivisions, other than school or institutional trust lands, that person shall obtain a permit from the division. The division may enter into memoranda of agreement to issue permits, project numbers, or to retain other data for federal lands and Native American lands within the state.
(b) Application for a permit shall be made on a form furnished by the section.
(c) The division shall make rules for the issuance of permits specifying or requiring:
(i) minimum permittee qualifications;
(ii)   duration;
(iii) for excavation permits, proof of permission from the landowner to enter the property for the purposes of the permit;
(iv) for excavation permits, research designs that provide for the recovery of the maximum amount of historic, scientific, archaeological, anthropological, and educational information, in addition to the physical recovery of specimens and the reporting of archaeological information meeting current standards of scientific rigor;
(v) the need, if any, to submit data obtained in the course of field investigations to the division;
(vi) proof of consultation with the appropriate Native American tribe, if necessary;
(vii) proof of consultation with the museum regarding curation of collections;
(viii) for excavation permits, proof of consultation with other agencies that may manage other legal interests in the land; and
(ix) other information the division considers necessary.
(d) All archaeological work shall be carried out under the supervision of the state archaeologist, which shall be under the direction of the director.
(e) A person may not remove from the state, prior to placement in a repository or curation facility, any specimen, site, or portion of any site from lands owned or controlled by the state or its subdivisions, other than school or institutional trust lands, without permission from the division, and prior consultation with the landowner and any other agencies managing other interests in the land.
(2) (a) Before any person may survey or excavate for archaeological resources on school or institutional trust lands, that person shall obtain a permit from the School and Institutional Trust Lands.

(b) The School and Institutional Trust Lands Administration may, by rule, delegate the authority to issue either survey or excavation permits, or both, for archaeological resources to the Division of State History.

(c) Application for a permit shall be made on a form furnished by the School and Institutional Trust Lands Administration.

(d) Issuance of a permit is an undertaking requiring consultation with the state historic preservation officer pursuant to Section **9-8-404**.

(e) The School and Institutional Trust Lands Administration shall enact rules for the issuance of permits specifying or requiring:

(i) minimum permittee qualifications;

(ii) duration;

(iii) the need to submit data obtained in the course of field investigations to the administration;

(iv) proof of consultation with the appropriate Native American tribe, if necessary;

(v) proof of consultation with the museum regarding curation of collections; and

(vi) other information the School and Institutional Trust Lands Administration considers necessary.

(f) A person may not remove from the state, prior to placement in a repository or curation facility, any specimen, site, or portion of any site from school or institutional trust lands without permission from the School and Institutional Trust Lands Administration, granted after consultation with the Division of State History.

(3) (a) Collections recovered from school and institutional trust lands shall be owned by the respective trust.

(b) Collections recovered from lands owned or controlled by the state or its subdivisions, other than school or institutional trust lands, shall be owned by the state.

(c) The repository or curation facility for collections from lands owned or controlled by the state or its subdivisions shall be designated pursuant to Section **53B-17-603**.

(4) The permitting agency may revoke or suspend a permit if the permittee fails to conduct a survey or excavation pursuant to law, the rules enacted by the permitting agency, or permit provisions.

(5) (a) Any person violating this section is guilty of a class B misdemeanor.

(b) A person convicted of violating this section, or the rules promulgated by the Division of State History or the School and Institutional Trust Lands Administration under this section, shall, in addition to any other penalties imposed, forfeit to the state or the respective trust all archaeological resources discovered by or through the person's efforts.

Amended by Chapter 170, 1995 General Session

The ancient Spanish inscription says "You are standing in quicksand, stupid".

Section 4:

READING SPANISH SYMBOLS

This is a good basic introduction on how to read Spanish treasure symbols. As always, there are many variations there of. On the trees that are still alive with these marks, they are very old and hard to see, so look hard. I've even painted some with white non-toxic paint so I can read them. When I was finished, I washed them off. Most symbols are not complete without the others that were meant to go with it. Usually you look off to the right of each symbol to get the next one. The Spanish were very smart and accurate. You need a good compass. Remember that true north has shifted a little since the 1700's.

This section on Spanish Treasure marks and mining symbols came from many sources, most of which I don't have information on who first printed them. Some came from a young man by the name of Stephen Shaffer. I spoke with him on the phone and got his permission to use some of his information. Thank you, Steve.

Two more 'Flower' symbols. These two symbols may look like each other at first glance but they are really two completely different symbols. One is showing a canyon, the ridges and just below and to the left of the top of the ridge is a mine. The petals indicate how many 'Varas' to proceed after reaching the head of the canyon, here the mine can be found. The other symbol is showing a canyon with two side knolls, and a large mountain at the head. The mine will be near one of the knolls. Notice how the flowers differ. When searching for symbols the flower symbol is most important if it is accompanied by a 'Notched' tree. If there is no notched tree then proceed ahead until one is found or another symbol is found.

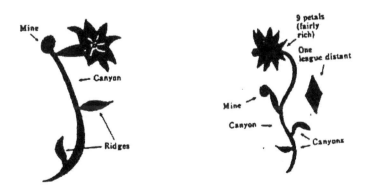

I thought of how Jim Bridger once told a prospector that there was a diamond on top of a mountain in the Yellowstone country which could be sighted fifty miles away "if a man got the right range on it when the sun was right." The prospector offered the old scout a fine horse and a new rifle if he would show it to him.

Notwithstanding the advantages of shadows, buriers of treasure have from time immemorial generally marked their deposits with signs that are directly visible, though usually quite enigmatical. The Spaniards, since they buried most of the treasure in this country, developed, of course, the most elaborate code of symbols. A register of these signs, collected and deciphered for the most part by a lawyer who refuses to allow the disclosure of his name, is now—for the first time, I believe—printed.

X   *On line to the treasure. X is also a common designation on landmarks.*

✝   *Cross and other rich objects pertaining to the Church are buried here.*

The cross might mean many things. So potent was its symbolism that the very sign of it might protect a man's possessions as well as himself. It often said: "I have been here"; "A Christian has passed this way." When Coronado went east in search of the Gran Quivira, he gave instructions that he was to be trailed by means of wooden crosses which he would erect from time to time along his route.

Slight change in course, to the left in this case.

On trail to wealth; Follow the long arm of the symbol.

This symbol is the meaning for 'Forest' or it's telling you to go into the trees for more symbols.

Distance Indicator Symbols

▬▬▬ ▬▬▬

Varas: Two.

▬ ▬▬ ▬▬ ▬

Trail: Correct line, continue.

— *A straight line indicates a certain number of varas to be measured off, the vara being 33⅓ inches; the number of varas called for usually ranges between 50 and 100.*

= *Two straight lines indicate double the distance of one line.*

△ *Triangle formed by trees or rocks enclosing treasure.*

▽ *Triangle formed by trees or rocks with treasure in the middle.*

△ *This sign indicates that while the deposit is marked by a triangle of trees or rocks, it is to be found to one side of the triangle.*

↷△ *Deposit is around a bend or curve away from triangle formed by trees or rocks.*

▭ *Treasure buried in box or chest.*

Mine shaft, tunnel or cave.

(1) In a tunnel.
(2) A tunnel with only one entrance.

(1) In a tunnel.
(2) A tunnel with two entrances.

Tunnel or shaft.

Peace pipe. Friendly Indians.

Sombrero, or hat. The number of sombreros shown indicates how many people were in the party that buried the treasure. The sombreros may also indicate the number of men killed by an enemy.

Mines close by. Any representation of the sun indicates proximity of mineral wealth.

O R O *Oro (gold) is short distance away.*

G *Gold short distance away.*

[*A tunnel.*

⟩ or ⟨ *Stop; change direction.*

⊕ or ⊕ *Perhaps variant signs of the cross.*

Greyhound. As to the meaning, there is some doubt.

Travel on, to a
triangle marked out
by trees or rocks.
Treasure will be at
one of the corners.

(1) Three varas deep.
(2) Proceed three varas.
(3) Treasure divided into three
parts, in boxes or chests.

*Flight of steps. This sign indicates that the treasure is down
in a cave or shaft.*

*Treasure is to be found within a triangle formed by trees
or rocks.*

*Over deposit, which is located within a triangle made by
trees or rocks.*

Living quarters

Kings mine

Change direction; Go
to your left around
the nearest hill. If
reversed, the trail
goes to the left.

Treasure is buried at the junction of
two streams farther on.

Treasure is buried in or near stream which is dry certain times of the year.

Proceed to nearby stream where you will find a waterfall. Cross at this point and continue in same direction.

This is the treasure site. (Location described at left on another marking.) Treasure is buried on the bank in the angle indicated by the dot or circle.

Treasure is buried in the middle of a stream; continue in same direction.

Treasure is buried in the middle of *this* stream. This is the treasure site.

Stream to be crossed at this point, then continue in direction indicated by the extended line (right).

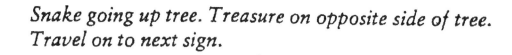 *Snake going up tree. Treasure on opposite side of tree. Travel on to next sign.*

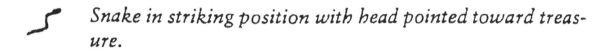 *Snake coming down tree. A snake or turtle coming down a tree means that treasure is on that side of it. Measure distance from the tip of the reptile's tail to the ground. Step off ten times that distance straight out. At the termination of the distance stepped, one should find either the treasure or another sign.*

Snake in striking position with head pointed toward treasure.

Snake coiled on tree or rock indicates presence of treasure directly beneath.

Coiled snake; Always follow the head.

Wrong way, change direction, Return to last marker

Ninus; Always follow the point.

(1) Treasure under.
(2) Mountain crest—dot indicating location of mine or treasure.

(1) Shaft or tunnel at foot of hill and center of hill.
(2) Shaft or tunnel in center of draw, meadow or valley.

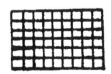

(1) Concealed opening.
(2) Concealed mine or cave.

Turtle with no legs;
Go no further, you
are at the treasure.

Head points toward treasure.
Continue straight ahead.

Feet close to the body;
Go ahead slowly, near
treasure.

Turtle with diamond back;
Count diamonds, if four, go
four varas or four leagues.

Turtle with head removed;
Treasure is gone, removed.

Turtle with tail curved;
Go in the direction of the
tail.

 Turtle, or dry land terrapin, with head pointing towards treasure. The turtle also means death, defeat, destruction, and the burial of possessions somewhere in the vicinity.

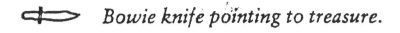 *Bowie knife pointing to treasure.*

Mule shoe lying horizontal: En route to treasure; keep traveling.

Mule shoe with toe down: Treasure is below.

Treasure directly underneath this sign.

Spanish gourd. On way to spring of water.

Direction Indicator; Follow the barrel of the hand gun. Usually found near a mine.

Dagger; Points to treasure or mine. If the blade is separated from the handle, it means to return to the last symbol and go in the opposite direction.

Cannon; Follow the Barrel of the Cannon, or go up the nearest canyon or hill.

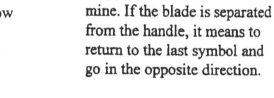

Direction Indicator; Follow the long arm but swing to the left.

Fish; Direction Indicator. Trail is next to or in a creek or on the edge of a lake.

This symbol is not only a direction indicator, but a symbol that means that a mine is close by. Also can mean mineral.

Gourd or Key; Follow the long arm.

120 Degrees

120 Degrees

—|—   *Horizontal cross. The long part of the upright points towards the treasure.*

—→   *Horizontal arrow without heft pointing towards treasure; sometimes towards water.*

↗   *Arrow without heft inclined upward pointing to other signs farther on.*

Travel around bend, away from second hill. Treasure buried where arc ends.

Treasure buried in lower half of hill.

Treasure buried between two small hills or knolls.

↘   *Arrow without heft pointing downward to treasure.*

↗   *Two or more arrows so connected indicate that treasure has been divided into as many parcels and buried in the directions pointed to.*

⇒   *Arrow with feathered heft flying away from mine or treasure.*

PLACER GOLD

Just a few nice photos showing the best places to look for gold in streams.

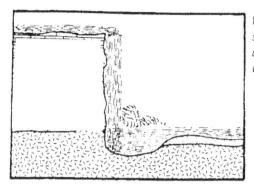

Waterfalls with considerable turbulence usually pulverize and wash out gold.

Waterfalls which have stream bed sand beneath them almost always concentrate gold.

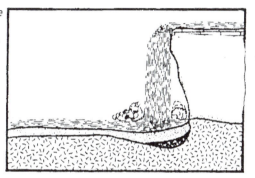

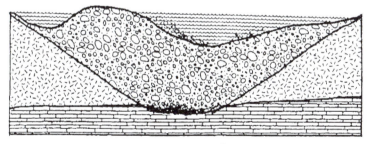

Sand bars often have a recent accumulation along the sides, but to get any quantity of gold, the best solution is to go to bedrock.

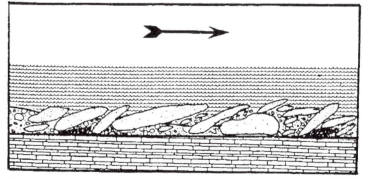

Rocks "shingle" on a stream bed near bedrock. An accumulation can be a good gold trap and many have given up a considerable amount of placer gold.

52

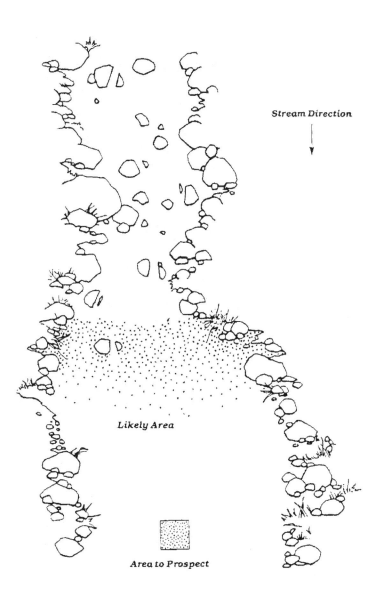

Stream Direction

Likely Area

Area to Prospect

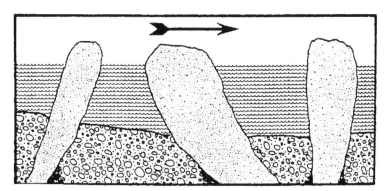

Boulders extending some distance into the stream bed are always worth investigating. Gold can accumulate downstream, upstream or on both sides, so take nothing for granted.

PLACER PAYDIRT

Points to remember: Look first to the obvious: large cracks, crevices, fissures (particularly those at points where the river or stream will slacken, or wide points, changes in direction, etc.), and the inside bends in the curves of the stream (more than likely associated with deposits of gravel). Observe areas where the river slows down for any reason (where the course of the river widens, after a set of rapids, deep pools in the riverbed or where the gradient dissipates thereby slowing flow). Check downstream from intersections of fault lines. Notice sections of river wherever the water current might slacken because of obstructions (boulders, outcroppings of bedrock, etc.). Be on the lookout for concentrations of black sand, old nails, horseshoes, etc. Sample depressions in rocks, particularly those that have many small boulders jammed into the depressions. Check and take a bucket of the material that is caught up in the tangle of exposed tree roots at the water's edge. Make notes of areas in the midsection of the stream where quantities of large boulders have drooped at the point at which the river or stream has widened. Pay attention to any area or condition that would have caused the carrying power of the stream to be reduced. Also look for large boulders that, although "beached" now, were at some time surrounded or completely submerged by a long-forgotten spring flood. Winter or early spring survey trips will reveal mid-stream boulders high and dry and easily accessible by mid-summer. It also pays to check out areas where there's evidence of placer tailings from the "old" days, where miners in the desire to cover as much ground as possible often exhibited "haste made waste" in their recovery methods.

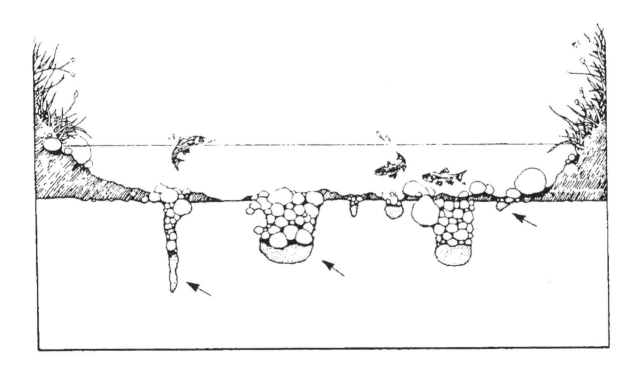

Section 6:

DOWSING

This subject is very interesting. It is a natural skill that can be developed by almost anyone. Use common sense and stay balanced in all your activities. I have seen many dozens of books on dowsing. Most were very confusing. The only one I ever saw that I could tune in to was by Ona Evers. I used some of her statements in this section because she worded them so perfectly. I could not change them, or think of a better way to say it. I would love to talk to her some day. I have been unable to find her.

Just what is dowsing, anyway? Basically, dowsing is searching. Searching for, among other things, under ground water (so-called water witching), minerals, oil, lost objects, people, information.

It is used quite matter-of-factly all over the world to locate underground cables, gas pipes, and water lines. Archeologists use dowsing to find hidden sites. Building industries use it to pin-point structural weaknesses. New uses for dowsing are constantly being discovered, and old uses revived. Although often surprising, dowsing is not weird or spooky. It is a useful art or skill that anyone can learn with practice.

Some persons grasp the art instantly- so fast that it's as if dowsing grasped them. They are the truly gifted ones. The rest of us have to try harder. Dowsing's as natural as memory.

In Europe, particularly in England and the Soviet Union, dowsing is used as a commonplace adjunct to archeology. Roman camps, druid ruins(in England), demolished palaces and old battle grounds (in Russia) are being reconstructed for modern eyes with information found by dowsing.

Meanwhile, millions of producing wells over the centuries have been dug, minerals and oil found through dowsing. So avoid the arguments. You'll never convince a true skeptic, no matter what.

If you follow the simple suggestions in these pages, and the L rods swing out like garden gates, then you are a strongly gifted dowser. I envy you, but not so much that it hurts. The rest of us, the weaker gifted, will be following right along.

Why should you even bother to learn to dowse it your gift is weak or almost zero? Because you want to . And because it's intriguing and fun, and useful. When you've developed the knack, you'll find it's as satisfying as an athletic endeavor or creative effort that foes just right. Dowsing can become the most absorbing hobby you've ever learned, or even a profitable vocation.

If you try the methods given in these pages, practice, and keep an open-mended venturesome spirit there is nothing to prevent your becoming a true dowser in a short time.

The Rods and Their Uses

Gold, silver, ivory, horn, rare woods, crowbars, snips of wire, fishing rods, keys, welding rods, nails, copper, nylon, maple, apple, peach, hazel, willow woods, whale bone, buttons, car radio antennae, blades of grass, plumb bobs, coat hangers, pendants and pliers- these are some of the materials and objects used in dowsing rods.

All of which means that the rod doesn't matter. It is you- the dowser- that matters. Many dowers use no rod at all. Just their hands. The rod is merely a pointer, an indicator like the needle of a compass. Something you can see. Any indicator which can be held in "unstable equilibrium" (13) will work. (I'm assuming that you're not quite in the Hand Dowser class yet.)

When describing them, most dowsers divide the fords into four main classifications:

1. The L rods, which are any rods that swing outward or inward as a recognizable signal - like the coat hangers.

2. The pendulum - which can be any object at all hung from a cord, or such like.

3. The bobber - a straight flexible stick, thicker at one end than on the other. When held by the thin end, its up-and-down bobbings are used for information - often something that is to be counted, or measured, such as distance or depth.

4. Last is the Y- shaped rod, the classical symbol of dowsing. It , too, can be made of any material. However, a flexible rod is felt to be more sensitive and easy to "read", although several the local dowsers use stiff and well-aged branches.

Any of the four rod types can be used in place of any of the others, depending on your preference.

The best way to get started is to get two L rods made of cast hangers or bent welding rods. Hold them like two six-guns. Hold them level and walk smoothly. Beforehand have someone hide something in your yard. Or you can look for your own water pipes. Practice on something you know is there. You might have to practice for a whole month before the rods swing out or in for you reliable . If you are gifted it will happen soon and with bigger movements. When the rods don't move, there is usually something blocking their action.   In the case of beginners, it is almost always simply a lack of concentration. We're letting thoughts from the conscious mind force their way in. Be patient. The knack will come.

Have you ever seen an artist squint up his eyes to blur things and fuzz out obtrusive details from the overall pattern of the of the scene before him? I've found this squinting is helpful in keeping my mental focus on the object of my search. However, if you feel you've lost the spirit of detached anticipation, stop. Dowsing is a skill that, for me at any rate, is best practiced in small frequent doses.

Many dowsers say it doesn't work for them unless there is a purpose to it, a certain importance in the hunt. Something they, or someone else, really needs. Obviously, there isn't much importance in finding what ever your friend hid for you in your yard. What is important is that you are searching for a new skill.

After you practice while and start to get fairly good you might be tempted to go show off for someone or take part in a test for science of t.v. never do it . For some reason it never works and you will be portrayed as an idiot.

Lets get back to a little practicing. Remember think of what you're looking for. Concentrate visually on the tip of whatever rod you're using, and either picture the object of your search, or ask, "Am I over a water line?" Or more specifically, "please tell me when I'm over a pipe with running water in it." Be polite to your rod. You will get exactly what you ask for .

Relax, focus only on the tip of the rod, expect nothing, but try to be athletically poised. Slowly the rod will swing around to point at the hidden cruet. And then, again, it may not. Don't be discouraged. The knack will come. Remember when practicing search for anything you can verify.

Don't forget you might get to what is called "learners Plateau". All of a sudden you don't get any reading at all. It happened to me. As I started to get the gang of it, I had become careless and hadn't really focused on the object of my search. Instead, I'd lit myself become tense all over, trying too hard. Every athlete, or creative person, knows that's the dumbest thing you can do. Teeth clenched, muscles tight, energies going in the wrong direction.

So unclench and think only of what you're looking for. And don't knot your brow about that either. Flow with it. Enjoy it. You don't have to dowse. No world shattering events will take place it you don't. No one is waiting, shovel in hand, for you to point out the spot for him to dig. I hope.

Remember that what ever makes dowsing work can be effected greatly by other people. Make sure you are not surrounded by negative people or noise and that you are not to tired. Always try to avoid all the fancy gadgets out there that are supposed to help you dowse better.

Keep your dowsing as simple and uncluttered as possible. Passive concentration is the watchword. Don't push against the river. Float.

PRINTED WORKS USED

Legends of Lost Missions and Mines - C. W. Polzer S. J.

Early Spanish Treasure Signs - W. Mahan

T. H. Northwest - Ruby Hult

Handbook of Treasure Signs - M. L. Carlson

Prospecting, Placer - Joe Petralia

Everybody's Dowser Book - Ona C. Evers

Treasure Monuments. Archives Assisted - C. A. Kenworthy

Principles and Practice of Radiesthesia - Abb Mermet

Reading Spanish Symbols - Stephen Shaffer

The next two chapters are related to the previous chapter on treasure marks. The next chapter is on mine trail markers/monuments. Read carefully. It may help you greatly next time you are out looking for treasure. This information is being used by permission from Chuck Kenworthy. I called him back in 1997 and talked with him. He was very nice. He has books out that go into even more detail on these subjects. The second chapter is on Spanish Death Traps. This is very important to know.

Section 7:

SPANISH TRAIL MONUMENTS

Introduction

Beginning in early 1983, we began receiving hundreds of drawings from archives that depicted the trail markers and monuments that Spain required to be built/constructed both into and out of mountain/hill ranges that contained a major mine or treasure.

I would venture to say that tens of thousands of Spanish treasure/mine trail monuments/ markers exist today in the United States. I have seen well over one thousand of them throughout our country as well as hundreds just over the border in Mexico. The King of Spain **ORDERED** all treasure/mine trails to be monumented according to Spain's drawings of markers/monuments. The Palace of Governors in Mexico City and Sante Fe (New Mexico) **INSTRUCTED** the exploration groups, haciendas, mining/explorers etc. in the basics of both monument meanings and map codes. **AFTER** a mine was established, the Palace of Governors would appoint two marker/monument building supervisors to oversee the actual construction. Additionally, the Palace appointed a map-maker and a "religious" from the nearby or adjoining cathedral to begin accompanying the hacienda/miners for the purpose of caring for the souls of the miners to, from and at the mine. Also, of course, these appointed "religious" had freedom to map Indian villages and convert natives they might encounter. Note: The Jesuits were firmly against Spain's use of natives as laborers because of Spain's extremely harsh treatment of native labor. The Jesuits expulsion from New Spain in 1767 was primarily caused by their opposition to Spain in this matter. Both Mexico City and Santa Fe regulated and enforced the King's rule, received the King's 15% to 20% fee from the haciendas/miners etc., required the trail monuments to be built so that if they wanted to "inspect/check" the operations without notice, they could easily find and follow the monumented trail into desolate mountainous terrain. Also, if all miners were to meet with some great disaster, the King of Spain could again located and re-establish the mine - or retrieve the hidden treasure by following the monumented trail.

Therefore, the trail markers to and from were required as well as treasure/mine maps. Note: All treasure/mine maps symbols/signs etc. were also identical in use and meaning throughout this New World. Also, a standard or special list of "measurements" were used on treasure/mine maps because Spain could not operate with hundreds of different codes, measurement and different monument/marker meanings when they were dealing with so many mines in the New World.

If we think about it for a minute, it becomes very clear that Spain was extremely wise

Foreword

This is a photobook of carved/cut Spanish markers and monuments on **TREASURE TRAILS** existing in these United States. Also their **MEANINGS** and how to **VERIFY** that they are not the work or design of **MOTHER NATURE** will be shown

Even though some of these **TREASURE TRAIL MARKERS/MONUMENTS** have been around for 300 years or so, they have not been recognized and are being shown and explained herein for the first time through both archival and in-the-field **RESEARCH**.

RECOGNIZING and **UNDERSTANDING** these trail **MARKERS** should be of significant interest to, **HISTORIANS, ARCHAEOLOGISTS, HIKERS, BACKPACKERS, COWBOYS, ROCKHOUNDS, HUNTERS OF LOST MINES AND TREASURES**, as well as any that might roam the deserts and mountains while **FISHING, HUNTING** or just **VACATIONING.**

Some of these Spanish monuments come close to rivaling those of **EGYPT** and **PERU** in their detail. Properly understanding the **MEANING** and of course, **RECOGNIZING** these **TREASURE TRAIL MONUMENTS**, could lead anyone, even someone driving a car, on his way toward one of the many **HIDDEN MINES OR TREASURES AS YET UNFOUND IN THESE UNITED STATES**

TREASURE TRAIL MARKERS and **MONUMENTS** were constructed according to Spain's official directions and instructions here in the new world. **THAT IS WHY THE MONUMENTS FOUND TODAY IN KANSAS AND KENTUCKY ARE INDENTICAL TO THE ONES EXISTING IN CALIFORNIA, ARIZONA, TEXAS, COLORADO, UTAH, NEW MEXICO, MEXICO, ETC., ETC., ETC.**

"A"

The Spanish had permanent campsites spaced along the rivers, streams and creeks they followed to reach their goal. In some cases their final camp was made at a **FRIENDLY INDIAN VILLAGE** where they would leave some of their cattle/sheep etc. to graze with a few peons to oversee and bring into the mine workers when needed. The friendly Indians would be paid for this accomodation in cattle etc. (mostly injured) when the group returned home. However, when possible, the final Spanish camp would be developed as close to the entrance of the range or desert as possible.

"A" Above; #1 is a major boulder **SHAPED INTO A BED** to indicate **"THIS IS A RESTING PLACE"** #2, the **RIGHT SIDE OF THE BED FORMS THE NUMBER "7"** (taken from the bible) **ON THE 7TH DAY HE RESTED.** #3 is an **ARROWHEAD SHAPED BOULDER** pointing to **WATER CLOSE BELOW.** Note the **HOLLOWED/CUPPED UPPER PORTION OF #3.** #4 is unrelated to this campsite. It is a **HEART** that directs toward **THE TRAIL HEAD ENTRANCE TO GOLD.**

"B" OPPOSITE PAGE, TOP PHOTO IS A CLOSE-UP OF THE BED, #7, THE CUPPED ARROWHEAD AND THE "HEART".

NOTE: IF YOU FIND/LOCATE A CAMPSITE YOU SHOULD SEARCH IT DILIGENTLY WITH METAL DETECTORS. MAJOR "FINDS" have been made at these old Spanish campsites, because usually, if not always, the **HIERARCHY AND OWNERS OF THE CAMP THAT WENT IN WITH THE MINERS WOULD HIDE/BURY AT THIS LAST CAMP.**

CAMP ALL OF THEIR "STREET CLOTHES, GOLD AND SILVER BUCKLES, GOLD AND SILVER COINS (needed for distant travel) GOLD JEWELRY AND FANCY KNIVES ETC. with the intent of picking them up on their way home. WELL, SOME NEVER MADE IT OUT OR AT LEAST NEVER PICKED UP WHAT THEY BURIED. We have "WORKED" every campsite that we have found and it has been very worthwhile. In 1985 about $170,000.00 was picked up, less than two feet deep at a campsite (not shown) about 10 miles from this one shown in "A" and "B".

"C" is another BED #1, #2's" are the BED SIDES, #3 is the HEADBOARD, #4 is the letter "V" that points to a FRAMED MAP THAT DIRECTS THE TOTAL WAY TO THE NEARBY MINE IN MAP CODE. This BED may not look too well designed from this close-up photo, but it was constructed to be seen from a distance, where it looks perfect in form.

"A" #1 is a **16 FOOT TALL** magnificently carved **"BIRD"** monument perched on a low ridgeline. It's "eyes" look and it's "beak" points to the large flat and wide pointer rock that shows "light" under it and is raised above ground level. If you remember your signs and symbols, you will recall that a bird sign/symbol on a "map" represents a change of direction. In the field, a "bird" means **"MANY"** changes of directions to come along this trail. The wide flat pointer on the rock the bird is looking at says: "Follow this canyon, **STAY** in the **WIDEST** canyon, do not turn off into any of the (many) narrow draws or canyons." The bird looking "**DOWN**" also tells us that the next marker will not be on a ridgeline--look for it to be "**LOW**" in this wide canyon.

"B" Is the classic and commonly used **BIRD** monument on most trails, and is easily constructed. It's meaning is **IDENTICAL** to photo "A", in that is says: "**THERE WILL BE MANY CHANGES OF DIRECTION ALONG THIS TRAIL, BE ALERT FOR MARKERS**".

On the opposite page are two photos of the same cross. Most trail crosses are simply carved/cut into cliff faces and large boulders along the **OUT** (homeward) **TRAIL**.

NOTE: Be very alert to the fact that a **CROSS** or a "T" (a **TOBIAS SYMBOL**) on a map means exactly the opposite of what a cross means when found in the field along trails.

#1 is a cross made by enlarging a cave or crack or actually digging it, which they probably did because of it's major messages and it's all important location. The **CROSS** itself just says that we are on the homeward trail.

#2 is a shaped 200 pound rock that serves two purposes. "A" This rock is wedged and cut to fit into the lower part of the cross and has a **POINT** that points down the curved bottom line of the cross saying **FOLLOW DOWN**. We follow down and the very bottom of the cross turns left **WITH A WIDE FLAT END.**

#3 is the message: **"TRAVEL DOWN FROM THIS POINT TO A LARGE FLAT AREA, THEN TURN TO THE LEFT INTO A CONTINUING WIDE FLAT AREA OR CANYON/ ON YOUR WAY HOMEWARD"**

--- OR "B":

#4 is a V shaped notch along the top line of rock #2.

#5 is a flat area made so that a person can sit and look through the notch #4 the same as you would look through the rear site of a rifle or place a spyglass in the notch.

#6 is a portion of the cliff face that has been cut away which now allows for sighting through notch #4 to see a **MAJOR OUT TRAIL MONUMENT** about a mile and a half away on a mountain slope.

#7 is the inverted "V" (refer to) which points to this trail "B" as being the best (and Royal) trail out.

"A"

A-1: IS OF COURSE A DIREC-TIONAL POINTER. IT POINTS TO POINT "2" OF A COMPASS TYPE ROCK TRIANGLE. THE DARK AREA IS A PART OF A CAVE EN-TRANCE THAT IS ABOUT EIGHT FEET DEEP. THE LARGE BOUL-DER TO THE RIGHT IS ABOUT 6 FEET OUT FROM THE CAVE EN-TRANCE. NOTE THE 3 ROCKS ABOVE THE POINTER, ONE IS ALMOST WHITE, POSSIBLY MEANT TO BE AN "EYE-CATCHER".

A-2: TO THE RIGHT OF NUMBER 2 IS POINT "2" OF THE TRI-ANGLE, SEE COMPASS ROCK PAGE FOR PHOTO. ABOUT ONE HOUR EACH WAY OF "HIGH NOON" IS THE ONLY TIME THAT SUN/SHADOW SIGNS CAN BE SEEN.
THE CREW MEMBER IS HOLD-ING A MAGNETOMETER DUR-ING OUR SURVEY.

"B"

B-1: IS AGAIN A POINTER, IN THIS IN-STANCE THE LONG ARM IS CUT SO DEEP THAT IT CAN BE SEEN ALMOST ALL DAY LONG AND LOOKS LIKE A NOR-MAL CRACK OR CREVICE. BUT NOTE THE ROCK THAT PROJECTS OUT AT THE TOP OF THE LONG CURVED ARM. AT HIGH NOON THE SUN CAUSES A SHADOW TO FALL BELOW THE ROCK AND FORM THE POINTER. THE MES-SAGE IS: "GO UP THE LARGE CREVICE, #2."

B-2: THIS WIDE CREVICE IS VERY STEEP, ABOUT 150 FEET UPWARD, AND I DON'T THINK ANYONE WOULD TRY TO CLIMB IT,--BUT IT'S EASY, IT HAS STEPS CUT INTO THE ROCK ALL THE WAY TO THE TOP, HOWEVER THE STEPS DON'T BE-GIN AT THE BOTTOM, THEY BEGIN ABOUT 10 FEET UP, AND THE BRUSH COMPLETELY HIDES THIS TRAIL OF STEPS.

This is a very large and detailed trailhead monument. #1 is the trail directional pointer. It's approximately a 2 1/2 ton rock held up by volleyball sized rocks to allow light/sky to shine through. #2 is a rock with a 90° notch indicating that this trail is a single trail, no choices. #3 is an **INDIAN HEAD** with a top knot, a warning to be alert along the trail. #4 is the top knot and #5 is the **HOLE**, the mine/treasure symbol. This monument says: the trail into the mountains begins here. It is a single trail and if problems arise, turn around and come out the way you went in. **BE ALERT**. This trail will probably encounter **INDIANS** before you reach your goal, the **"HOLE"**.

O.K., that's all the treasure- now drop the rope down to me, Burt.....Burt....Burt!

Section 8:

DEATH TRAPS

Foreword

THE ONLY GOOD THING, OR RATHER, POSITIVE ASPECT RELATED TO DISCOVERING A "DEATH TRAP" IS THE ABSOLUTE CONFIRMATION THAT YOU HAVE "BROKEN THE MAP'S CODE CORRECTLY" OR FOLLOWED THE INSTRUCTIONS PROPERLY — FOR YOU ASSUREDLY ARE IN THE IMMEDIATE AREA OF A MAJOR MINE OR TREASURE, OR POSSIBLY BOTH. TUNNELS OF RICH MINES ARE KNOWN TO HAVE BEEN FILLED WITH TREASURES PRIOR TO THE COVERING AND CONCEALING OF THE MINE ITSELF.

BY FAR, THE MAJORITY OF ALL SPANISH DEATH TRAPS ARE IN THE IMMEDIATE "AREA" OF THE ENTRANCE TO THE MINE/TREAS- URE AND **NOT WITHIN THE MINE OR TREASURE ROOM ITSELF.**

SUBTLE AND MAN MADE CHANGES WERE MADE IN TOPOGRAPHY, MARKINGS INSCRIBED ON BOULDERS, LARGE ROCKS "AR- RANGED", BOULDERS "RESHAPED", ETC., IN THE IMMEDIATE "ENTRANCE" AREA. THESE WERE SET-UP TO "ENTICE/ACT AS A MAGNET", TO MISLEAD AND BEGUILE ANYONE WHO WAS CLEVER ENOUGH TO GET WITHIN A COUPLE OF HUNDRED FEET OF THE ACTUAL "ENTRANCE" AND DRAW HIM AWAY FROM THE "JACKPOT" AND TO ONE OF THE NEARBY DEATH TRAP LOCATIONS.

STUDY THE DEATH TRAPS AND **COMMIT THE TRAP WARNING SIGNS AND SYMBOLS TO MEMORY.** YOUR KNOWLEDGE AND MEMORY MAY SAVE A LIFE, POSSIBLY YOUR OWN. WHAT COULD BE WORSE THAN SPENDING MANY YEARS OF SEARCHING, AND THEN, WHEN WITHIN "A STONE'S THROW" OF YOUR GOAL — YOU GET SUCKER PUNCHED.

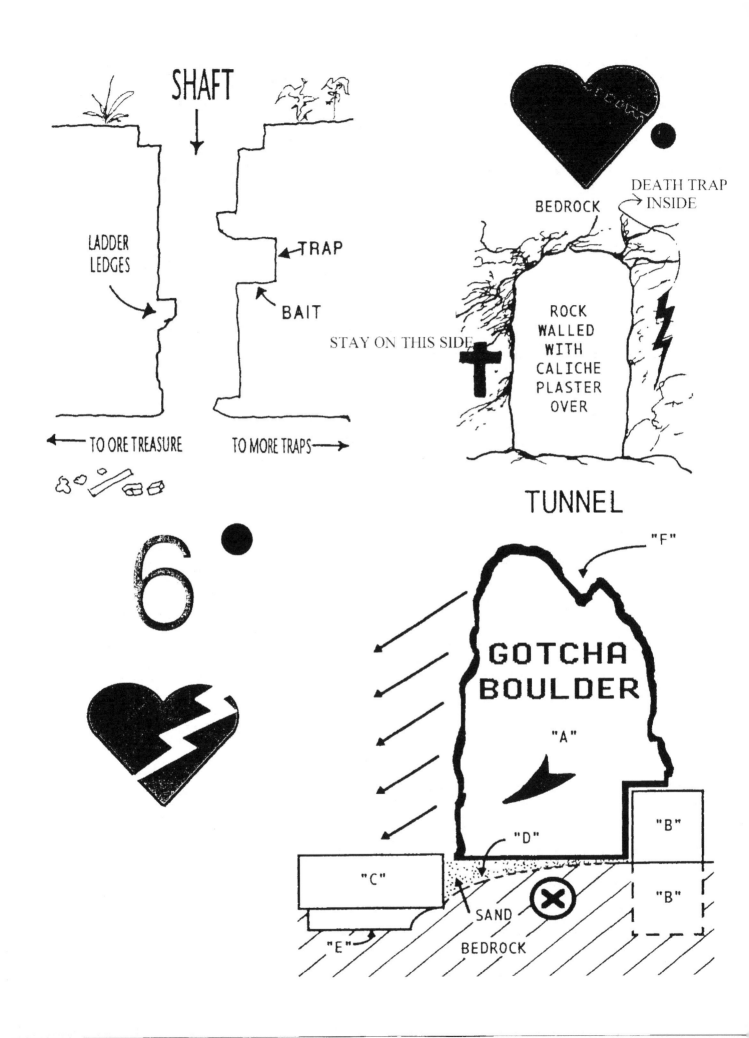

SHAFT

LADDER LEDGES

TRAP

BAIT

STAY ON THIS SIDE

BEDROCK

DEATH TRAP INSIDE

ROCK WALLED WITH CALICHE PLASTER OVER

← TO ORE TREASURE

TO MORE TRAPS →

TUNNEL

6°

"F"

GOTCHA BOULDER

"A"

"D"

"B"

"C"

"B"

SAND

"E"

BEDROCK

THIS IS THE "DEATH TRAP GRANDE", THE MOST COMMON TRAP FREQUENTLY USED BY THE SPANISH. THIS TRAP WAS DESIGNED TO CRUSH EIGHT TO FIFTEEN SEARCHERS AT ONCE.

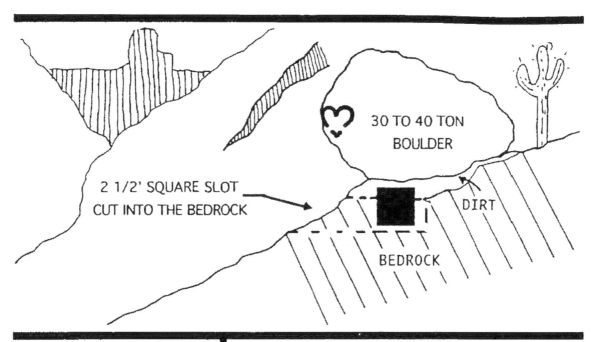

30 TO 40 TON BOULDER

2 1/2' SQUARE SLOT CUT INTO THE BEDROCK

DIRT

BEDROCK

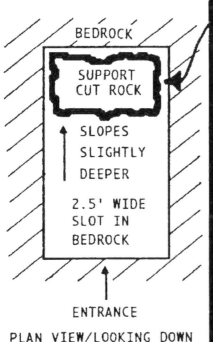

BEDROCK

SUPPORT CUT ROCK

SLOPES SLIGHTLY DEEPER

2.5' WIDE SLOT IN BEDROCK

ENTRANCE

PLAN VIEW/LOOKING DOWN

THIS ROCK WAS CUT TO FIT INTO THE "SLOT" VERY TIGHTLY AND PLACED AGAINST THE BACK WALL OF THE SLOT FOR FURTHER UPRIGHT SUPPORT AS WELL AS SUPPORT OF NOT MOVING OR FALLING "BACKWARDS" DURING A "TEMBLOR" (EARTHQUAKE) OR OTHER MAJOR LAND DISTURBANCE. THESE "SUPPORT ROCKS" **ALWAYS MUST PROJECT TWELVE (12) TO EIGHTEEN (18) INCHES ABOVE THE SIDES OF THE BEDROCK WALLS WITH THE BOULDER RESTING ON IT.**

DIRECTLY BELOW THE POINTER OF THE BROKEN HEART WILL BE THE "ENTRANCE" OR BEGINNING OF THE SLOT CUT INTO THE BEDROCK AND

SLOT CUT INTO THE BEDROCK AND USUALLY FOUND ONLY ABOUT A FOOT OR SO UNDER THE SURFACE OF THE GROUND ON THE SLOPE.

WHEN YOU FIND ONE OF THESE DON'T DO AS WE HAVE DONE AND CHIP AWAY AT THE SUPPORT ROCK THINKING IT IS JUST A "CAP ROCK" THAT SEALS THE ENTRANCE TO THE TREASURE ROOM OR MINE. IT SURELY DOESN'T LOOK LIKE A "TRAP"—IT LOOKS LIKE A MOST PERFECT PLACE AND WAY TO "HIDE/CONCEAL" AN ENTRANCE TO A MINE/TREASURE. ALSO, HOW COULD SUCH A SMALL 2-1/2 SQUARE FOOT ROCK HOLD UP A 30 to 40 TON BOULDER 25' WIDE BY 12' DEEP AND 9' TALL — AND AFTER ALL, DIDN'T THE BOULDER HAVE A HEART, THE SPANISH SYMBOL FOR GOLD, CARVED INTO ITS FACE?

THIS GRANDE TRAP IS ONE OF THE FULLY EXPOSED TRAPS THAT SITS IN TOTALLY INOCENT VIEW. WHEN THE BOULDER IS RELEASED THE WORKERS AND WATCHERS ON THE LOWER SIDE ARE IMMEDIATELY CRUSHED. ADDITIONALLY, AND ESPECIALLY IF THIS TRAP IS HIGH ON A MOUNTAINSIDE SLOPE, THIS BOULDER'S ROAR DOWN HILL WILL TEAR A PATH TWENTY FIVE FEET WIDE AND A FEW FEET DEEP POSSIBLY CATCHING A FEW MORE LAID BACK INTRUDERS.

EVEN IF THIS GRANDE BOULDER DOES NOT STRIKE ANOTHER INTRUDER ON IT'S RUSH DOWNHILL, THE NOISE IT MAKES AND THE PATH IT CUTS WILL SURELY PUT THE FEAR OF GOD — OR OF THE SPANISH, INTO THE HEARTS OF ANY UNTOUCHED INTRUDERS.

SPAIN'S COMMENTS ON THIS ADDED MENTAL IMPACT IS THAT "IT MAY WELL BE ENOUGH TO CAUSE THE REMAINING INTRUDERS TO ABANDON THEIR SEARCH AND RAPIDLY DEPART THE AREA SAYING A PRAYER OF THANKSGIVING TO THEIR PAGAN GODS."

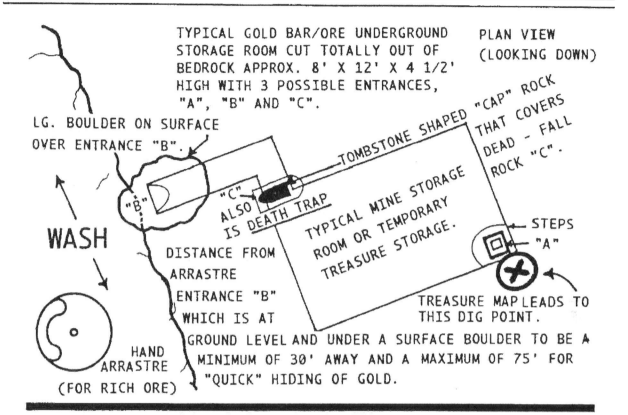

TYPICAL GOLD BAR/ORE UNDERGROUND STORAGE ROOM CUT TOTALLY OUT OF BEDROCK APPROX. 8' X 12' X 4 1/2' HIGH WITH 3 POSSIBLE ENTRANCES, "A", "B" AND "C".

PLAN VIEW (LOOKING DOWN)

LG. BOULDER ON SURFACE OVER ENTRANCE "B".

TOMBSTONE SHAPED "CAP" ROCK THAT COVERS DEAD – FALL ROCK "C".

"C" ALSO IS DEATH TRAP

TYPICAL MINE STORAGE ROOM OR TEMPORARY TREASURE STORAGE.

WASH

"B"

STEPS "A"

DISTANCE FROM ARRASTRE ENTRANCE "B" WHICH IS AT

TREASURE MAP LEADS TO THIS DIG POINT.

HAND ARRASTRE (FOR RICH ORE)

GROUND LEVEL AND UNDER A SURFACE BOULDER TO BE A MINIMUM OF 30' AWAY AND A MAXIMUM OF 75' FOR "QUICK" HIDING OF GOLD.

EVERY GOLD MINE THAT CONTAINED RICH POCKETS OF VISIBLE AND SIZABLE GOLD NORMALLY HAD A "GOLD ROOM" WITH A "HAND ARRASTRE" WITHIN 75 FEET. ANOTHER "GOLD ROOM" WAS ALWAYS AT THE HACIENDA'S (OWNER'S) PERMANENT **CAMPSITE** WHICH COULD BE SOME DISTANCE AWAY BUT BETTER PROTECTED. THE GOLD ROOM WITH THE ARRASTRE IS ALWAYS AT LEAST 1/4 LEAGUE (1/2 MILE) BELOW OR AWAY FROM THE MINE ITSELF, NORMALLY IN A SIDE CANYON WASH (FAULTLINE) WITH INTERMITTENT EXPOSED BEDROCK ALONG AT LEAST ONE SIDE AND ITS BOTTOM. THE HAND ARRASTRE IS CUT INTO A SIDE OF THE BEDROCK WASH IN SUCH A LOCATION THAT THE FLOWING WATER FROM THE SPRING HIGHER UP OR THE DRAINING RAINFALL WATER IN THE WASH CAN BE DIRECTED INTO AND CAN FLOW THROUGH THE ARRASTRE BOWL. 3 TO 5 MEN SIT AND HOLD ORE IN ONE HAND AND STRIKE THE MATRIX WITH A HAMMER AND BREAK IT UP. THE BOTTOM CENTER OF THE BOWL HAS ABOUT A 4" DIAMETER HOLE ABOUT 4" DEEP, ABOUT THE SIZE OF A "HOLE OR CUP" ON A GOLF COURSE TO CATCH OR HOLD THE HEAVY MATERIAL (GOLD).

NORMALLY I'M NOT SHOWING SIMILAR DEATH TRAPS IN THIS BOOK. HOWEVER, THIS ONE IS UNIQUE BECAUSE OF ITS **"BAIT OF GOLD"** AND POPULARITY WITH THE SPANISH. IT WAS USED IN **SHAFT WALL** CAVES FOR SHAFT PLUG TRAPS BUT INSTALLED MAINLY IN TUNNELS AND AT THE END OF PASSAGEWAYS.

THE WOODEN BOX MUST HAVE A LID AND HANDLES ON THE THREE EXPOSED SIDES. ALSO THE BOX SHOULD BE AT LEAST 3-1/2 FEET WIDE AND OF COURSE WIDER THAN THE BASE OF THE GOTCHA BOULDER.

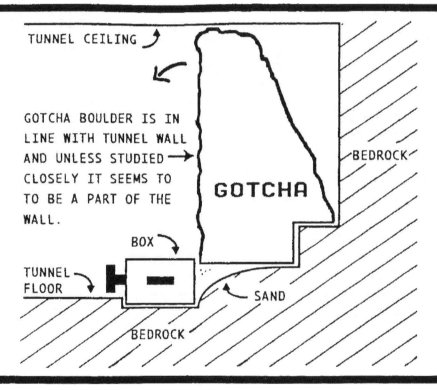

THE BOX IS SET IN A RECESSED AREA OF THE BEDROCK FLOOR. THE HANDLES ASSIST IN THE MOVING/PICKING-UP OF THE BOX WHICH HAS ABOUT 100 POUNDS OF GOLD ORE WITH MAYBE A SPECIMEN PIECE OR TWO IN READY VIEW.

UPON MOVING THE BOX, THE SAND THAT HAS BEEN THE PARTIAL BASE FOR THE GOTCHA BOULDER IN CONJUNCTION WITH THE BACK WALL OF THE BOX IS RELEASED AND THE GOTCHA TOPPLES DOWN.

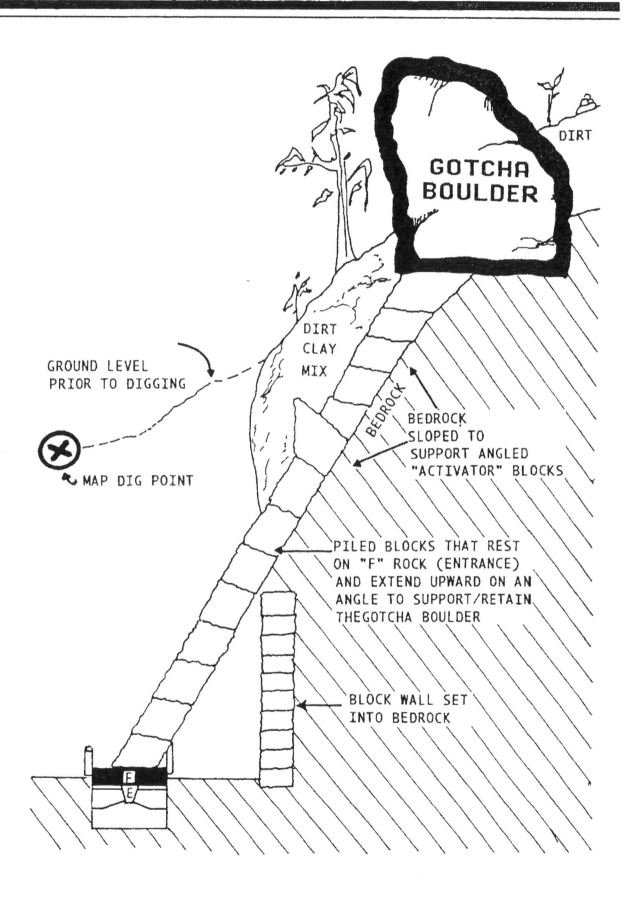

GOTCHA BOULDER

DIRT

DIRT CLAY MIX

BEDROCK

GROUND LEVEL PRIOR TO DIGGING

MAP DIG POINT

BEDROCK SLOPED TO SUPPORT ANGLED "ACTIVATOR" BLOCKS

PILED BLOCKS THAT REST ON "F" ROCK (ENTRANCE) AND EXTEND UPWARD ON AN ANGLE TO SUPPORT/RETAIN THEGOTCHA BOULDER

BLOCK WALL SET INTO BEDROCK

Made in the USA
Charleston, SC
25 June 2013